"IT'S LIGHTS OUT AND AWAY WE GO!"

Since the very first race of the World Championship of Drivers at Silverstone in 1950, Formula 1 drivers have pushed themselves to the limits both mentally and physically in their quest for glory. In one of the most exciting, demanding and dangerous sports in the world, only the very best can hope to reach the pinnacle of motorsport. Inside we celebrate Formula 1's most iconic drivers from the past 75 years – from the early pioneers of Alberto Ascari and Juan Manuel Fangio and the golden era racers of Niki Lauda, Jackie Stewart and James Hunt to the legendary rivals Ayrton Senna and Alain Prost and today's modern greats, including Lewis Hamilton and Max Verstappen, you'll discover a host of fascinating facts, stories and records about your favourite F1 stars.
We also run down the ten best Formula 1 races in history, as well as the most iconic circuits, top teams and more.
Enjoy the ride!

FORMULA 1 ALL-STARS

CONTENTS

- **6** LEWIS HAMILTON
- **10** JUAN MANUEL FANGIO
- **12** OSCAR PIASTRI
- **14** NELSON PIQUET
- **16** MICHAEL SCHUMACHER
- **20** CARLOS SAINZ
- **22** GRAHAM HILL
- **24** GEORGE RUSSELL
- **28** TOP 10 F1 RACES
- **30** AYRTON SENNA
- **34** NICO ROSBERG
- **36** ALBERTO ASCARI
- **38** LANDO NORRIS
- **42** NIKI LAUDA
- **44** JACQUES VILLENEUVE
- **46** FERNANDO ALONSO
- **50** TOP 10 F1 CIRCUITS
- **51** POSTERS
- **68** MAX VERSTAPPEN
- **72** JAMES HUNT
- **74** DANIEL RICCIARDO
- **76** KIMI RÄIKKÖNEN
- **78** ALAIN PROST

CONTENTS

46	
112	
28	
20	
102	
12	
24	

82	SERGIO PÉREZ
84	JACKIE STEWART
86	**TOP 10 F1 TEAMS**
88	CHARLES LECLERC
92	JIM CLARK
94	KIMI ANTONELLI
96	JACK BRABHAM
98	SEBASTIAN VETTEL
102	MIKA HÄKKINEN
104	RUBENS BARRICHELLO
106	JENSON BUTTON
108	NIGEL MANSELL
112	**TOP 10 F1 BOSSES**

FORMULA 1 ALL-STARS

Undeniably **THE MOST RECORD-BREAKING DRIVER** Formula 1 has ever known, Lewis Hamilton's career remains **UNRIVALLED ON THE TRACK**

LEWIS HAMILTON

As a seven-time World Champion, Lewis Hamilton is one of the most decorated and record-breaking racers in F1 history. Bursting onto the scene in 2007 with McLaren, the karting wonderkid from Stevenage quickly established himself as a force to be reckoned with, narrowly missing out on the Drivers' Championship in his rookie year. Undeterred, he claimed his first title a year later in dramatic fashion, winning by a single point.

Joining Mercedes in 2013, Hamilton went on to forge a reputation for fearless racing, precision and consistency that saw him dominate the hybrid era of Formula 1, and become the most successful driver ever with 105 wins and 202 podiums, ultimately redefining what is possible in the sport.

Off the track, Hamilton has been equally influential – a passionate advocate for diversity, sustainability and animal welfare, the vegan and fashion icon uses his platform to inspire change, cementing his legacy as a trailblazer transcending motorsport. What's more, he's received dozens of other prestigious accolades, including a knighthood and the BBC's Sport's Personality of the Year, which he won twice.

FAST FACT
Hamilton started racing aged eight and won the British karting championship (cadet class) and STP karting championship two years later.

LEWIS HAMILTON

Hamilton waves to the crowd after his final Mercedes race in Abu Dhabi, ending a record-breaking partnership

BIO

DATE OF BIRTH: 7 January 1985
BIRTHPLACE: Stevenage, England
NATIONALITY: British
YEARS ACTIVE: 2007-present
TEAMS: McLaren (2007-12), Mercedes (2013-24), Ferrari (2025-present)
FIRST ENTRY: 2007 Australian Grand Prix

F1 CAREER

7 F1 Championships (2008, 2014, 2015, 2017, 2018, 2019, 2020)
105 wins
202 podiums
104 pole positions

STATS & RECORDS

246 – Most races with a single constructor (with Mercedes, 84 of which were wins)

9 – Most wins at the same Grand Prix (British GP)

176 – Most front row starts

IMAGES: ADOBE STOCK, GETTY

FORMULA 1 ALL-STARS

DID YOU KNOW?
Lewis Hamilton became a Sir on the 15 December 2021 when he was knighted by the then Prince of Wales, now King Charles III.

THE DECIDER IN THE DESERT

>>> The 2021 Drivers' Championship saw Hamilton's rivalry with Max Verstappen explode during the season's controversial finale in Abu Dhabi. A late safety car led to race director Michael Masi allowing only some lapped cars to un-lap, setting up a dramatic final-lap showdown where Verstappen, on fresher tyres, overtook Hamilton to claim his first title. An FIA inquiry found gross inconsistencies in the safety car procedure, which led to rule changes and Masi's removal, but the decision to uphold Verstappen's championship victory is still considered to be widely controversial to this day.

THE LAST CORNER CLINCHER

> "Hamilton and Verstappen collided in spectacular fashion"

>>> The 2008 F1 finale at Brazil's Interlagos circuit, saw home talent Felipe Massa chasing his first title. Rain caused chaos, with tyre changes and crashes reshuffling the field, but Massa, who had enjoyed his best ever season crossed the line as champion, triggering celebrations, but the race wasn't over. On the final corner, Hamilton overtook Glock, whose tyres faltered in the rain, securing fifth place – all he needed to clinch the title by a single point, rewarding him with his first of seven championships.

IMAGES: ADOBE STOCK, GETTY

LEWIS HAMILTON

A CLOSE SHAVE

›› During lap 26 of the 2021 Italian Grand Prix, Hamilton and Verstappen collided in spectacular fashion at Monza's Turn 1 after rejoining the track side by side following pit stops. Verstappen's car was launched over Hamilton's, where its rear tyre rolled over Hamilton's helmet. Speculation suggests that without the halo device, the Brit could have suffered fatal injuries. Both drivers retired, and Verstappen was later penalised as the stewards deemed him predominantly at fault, further intensifying their championship rivalry.

HAMILTON'S FERRARI GAMBLE

›› In a seismic shift within Formula 1, Lewis Hamilton announced on 1 February 2024 that he would be leaving Mercedes to join Scuderia Ferrari for the 2025 season, ending a 12-year tenure that saw him clinch six of his seven titles. Calling it "one of the hardest" decisions he'd ever made, Hamilton admitted leaving Mercedes was emotional. However, after testing Ferrari's SF-25, he declared, "There is magic here." He teams up with Charles Leclerc, aiming to end Ferrari's title drought, which dates back to 2007.

FORMULA 1 ALL-STARS

Acclaimed by the likes of Hamilton and Schumacher as the GREATEST DRIVER OF ALL TIME, the Argentine legend was one of F1'S EARLIEST PIONEERS

JUAN MANUEL FANGIO

FAST FACT
As a teenager, Fangio almost died of pneumonia – he was bedridden for two months.

34
JUAN MANUEL FANGIO

FOUR TEAMS, FIVE TITLES

At first glance it appears that Fangio hopped from team to team looking for the best car, but the truth is more complicated. He left Alfa Romeo after winning his first world title because they pulled out of F1. He left Mercedes because they withdrew from F1 after the 1955 tragedy at Le Mans, he left Ferrari because he despaired of the politics, and returned to spiritual home Maserati for his final triumph in the legendary 1 (left).

It seems bizarre to racing fans today, but in 1952, the defending World Champion driver was left without a car. Juan Manuel Fangio had burst onto the F1 scene in 1950 and by 1951 he had claimed his first title. But Alfa Romeo, the dominant marque at the time, withdrew from the 1952 F1 season as they hadn't developed a car which would meet that year's specifications. Thereafter, Fangio continued to swap teams, but whoever he drove for, he made their cars competitive, displaying a remarkable ability to nurse cars with technical problems around a circuit more smoothly than any other driver. He used to say that he tried to win races at the slowest possible speed to preserve the cars' engines and tyres. An exception was the 1957 German Grand Prix, when he had to make up 50 seconds on the race leaders in order to win his fifth and final world title – a figure only surpassed by Lewis Hamilton and Michael Schumacher.

BIO

DATE OF BIRTH: 24 June 1911
BIRTHPLACE: Balcarce, Argentina
NATIONALITY: Argentinian
YEARS ACTIVE: 1950-51, 1953-58
TEAMS: Alfa Romeo (1950-51), Maserati (1953-54), Mercedes (1954-55), Ferrari (1956), Maserati (1957-58)
FIRST ENTRY: 1950 British Grand Prix

F1 CAREER

5 F1 Championships (1951, 1954, 1955, 1956, 1957)
24 wins
35 podiums
29 pole positions

STATS & RECORDS

51 – total starts
38 – the age at which Fangio started his F1 career
47.06% – highest percentage of race wins from starts (24 from 51)

FORMULA 1 ALL-STARS

Meet the CONTROVERSIAL BRAZILIAN and THREE-TIME DRIVERS' CHAMPION

NELSON PIQUET

After impressing in a handful of drives for minor teams in 1978, Piquet was snapped up by Brabham to race in the season finale and stayed for the next seven years. He transformed Bernie Ecclestone's outfit into championship contenders, snatching the Drivers' Championship from Carlos Reutemann at the final race of the 1981 season. Piquet repeated the feat two years later, this time stealing the trophy from under Alain Prost's nose. Aware that the notoriously frugal Ecclestone was paying him a fraction of what he was worth, Piquet jumped ship to Williams. However, he soon clashed with new teammate Nigel Mansell. As a double World Champion, Piquet thought he deserved a respect that Mansell did not show, and their infighting probably gifted the 1986 title to Prost. Piquet made amends when his consistency allowed him to cruise to the title in 1987 despite winning only three races to Mansell's six.

FAST FACT
Piquet had three F1 Grand Slams – achieved when a driver wins a Grand Prix from pole, leads every lap and sets the fastest lap of the race.

NELSON PIQUET

UNLIKELY RESULT IN LAS VEGAS

Piquet was one point behind Carlos Reutemann going into the last race of the 1981 season, but Reutemann's lacklustre showing gave Piquet a chance to win. Piquet himself only finished fifth, but the two points he gained was enough to leapfrog Reutemann in one of the closest finishes in championship history.

BIO

DATE OF BIRTH: 17 August 1952
BIRTHPLACE: Rio de Janeiro, Brazil
NATIONALITY: Brazilian
YEARS ACTIVE: 1978-91
TEAMS: Ensign (1978), BS Fabrications (1978), Brabham (1978-85), Williams (1986-87), Lotus (1988-89), Benetton (1990-91)
FIRST ENTRY: 1978 German Grand Prix

F1 CAREER

3 F1 Championships (1981, 1983, 1987)

23 wins

60 podiums

24 pole positions

STATS & RECORDS

9 – consecutive podium finishes in 1987

49.02% – percentage of point-scoring races

8 – consecutive seasons with a race win

IMAGES: ADOBE STOCK, GETTY

FORMULA 1 ALL-STARS

The German was the driver English fans LOVED TO HATE, but BOY WAS HE GOOD

MICHAEL SCHUMACHER

Michael Schumacher is one of the greatest F1 drivers the world has ever seen. His ability to push a car to its limits (and beyond them) was legendary, as was his attention to detail, his skill at producing a very fast lap when it was most needed, and his dedication to a punishing personal fitness regime which he believed would give him an edge. He could galvanise a team around him, and they in turn appreciated how hard he worked and his willingness to adapt to new technologies as they came along. Incredibly, Schumacher's feats have been eclipsed much sooner than we expected, by Lewis Hamilton. But the German genius will always stand high in the pantheon of great Formula 1 drivers and there's little doubt that, but for his tragic skiing accident, he would have continued to exert his influence on the sport even after his retirement as a driver.

FAST FACT
He was the guiding hand behind the 1994 relaunch of the Grand Prix Drivers' Association.

MICHAEL SCHUMACHER
47

Schumacher leads Juan Pablo Montoya at the Malaysian Grand Prix, one of 13 races (out of 18) he won in 2004

BIO

DATE OF BIRTH: 3 January 1969
BIRTHPLACE: Hürth, Germany
NATIONALITY: German
YEARS ACTIVE: 1991-2006, 2010-2012
TEAMS: Jordan (1991), Benetton (1991-95), Ferrari (1996-2006), Mercedes (2010-12)
FIRST ENTRY: 1991 Belgian Grand Prix

F1 CAREER

7 F1 Championships (1994, 1995, 2000, 2001, 2002, 2003, 2004)

91 wins

155 podiums

68 pole positions

STATS & RECORDS

29.55% – percentage of wins from race entries

51 – most wins not starting from pole position

15 – most consecutive seasons with a Grand Prix victory (jointly with Hamilton)

IMAGES: ADOBE STOCK, GETTY

FORMULA 1 ALL-STARS

DID YOU KNOW?
In 2004, he was voted Germany's greatest sportsperson of the 20th century.

FIRST WORLD TITLE

⟫⟫ Schumacher secured his first World Championship in 1994 by what some considered dubious, even nefarious, means. Irked, no doubt, by perceived unfair treatment from the authorities which led to him serving a two-race ban and suffering a further disqualification that year, Schumacher made sure his error in driving into a guardrail in the final race of the season did not cost him the title when, on re-joining the track, he turned into Damon Hill's car and forced the Englishman to retire.

CONTROVERSY WITH VILLENEUVE

⟫⟫ As was the case three years earlier, in 1997 Schumacher did not have the best car on the grid. Far from it. And yet his supreme talent allowed him to remain competitive the whole season. In the final race, in Jerez, Schumacher tried to take Jacques Villeneuve out of the race to protect his championship lead. On this occasion it failed, but the Canadian was in no doubt that it was a deliberate manoeuvre.

IMAGES: GETTY

MICHAEL SCHUMACHER

RECORD SEVENTH WORLD TITLE

>>> When Schumacher claimed his record-breaking seventh World Championship, it was his fifth in a row and he was quite clearly the most dominant driver for the whole of that time. His genius lay not only in a remarkable ability to push his Ferrari to its absolute limits, but in building a team around him that was as focused on winning as he was.

> "Part of his genius lay in his ability to push his Ferrari to its limits"

SKIING ACCIDENT

>>> Schumacher was an experienced skier but in 2013 he had a fall near Méribel in France while skiing with his then 14-year-old son, Mick. A serious head injury required surgery and, briefly, a medically induced coma to allow him to recover. Since then his true medical status has been a well-guarded secret, and he has not been seen in public, though reportedly he was able to attend daughter Gina-Maria's wedding in September 2024.

FORMULA 1 ALL-STARS

Known as **'CHILLI' FOR HIS FIERY DETERMINATION,** Carlos Sainz combines **INTELLIGENCE WITH INSTINCT**

CARLOS SAINZ

Born into racing royalty, Carlos Sainz Jr, son of two-time World Rally Champion Carlos Sainz Sr, has carved out his own legacy. After winning the Formula Renault NEC title in 2011 and the Formula Renault 3.5 Championship in 2014, he made his F1 debut in 2015 with Toro Rosso.

A consistent and determined performer, the Spaniard moved to Renault in 2017 before joining McLaren in 2019, where he claimed his maiden podium at the Brazilian Grand Prix. In 2021, Sainz transitioned to Ferrari, replacing Sebastian Vettel, and over the next four seasons secured four victories, including his first at the 2022 British Grand Prix and a standout triumph at the 2024 Mexico City Grand Prix.

In 2025, Sainz began a new chapter with Williams, partnering Alex Albon and bringing his experience and determination to drive the team forward.

FAST FACT
As '5' was already taken, Sainz doubled it to 55, which matches the two 'S's in his name.

CARLOS SAINZ JNR

SAINZ SUCCEEDS AT SILVERSTONE

Sainz's first Formula 1 victory came at the 2022 British Grand Prix, marking a defining moment in his career. Starting from pole position, Sainz navigated intense pressure and late-race drama, including a critical safety car restart, to overtake teammate Charles Leclerc. Displaying impeccable strategy and composure, he fended off challengers to cross the line first, becoming only the second Spanish driver to claim an F1 win – solidifying his place among the sport's elite.

BIO

DATE OF BIRTH: 1 September 1994

BIRTHPLACE: Madrid, Spain

NATIONALITY: Spanish

YEARS ACTIVE: 2015-present

TEAMS: Toro Rosso (2015-17), Renault (2017-18), McLaren (2019-20), Ferrari (2021-24), Williams (2025-present)

FIRST ENTRY: 2015 Australian Grand Prix

F1 CAREER

0 F1 Championships

4 wins

27 podiums

6 pole positions

STATS & RECORDS

1272.5 – fifth-most points without being World Champion

6.18 – average points per Grand Prix

4 – fastest laps

IMAGES: ADOBE STOCK, GETTY

FORMULA 1 ALL-STARS

FAST FACT
Graham and Damon Hill were the first of three father-and-son duos to become F1 champions.

GRAHAM HILL

Hill was a working-class engineer but his **MOVIE-STAR GOOD LOOKS AND STYLE** brought him fame

14 GRAHAM HILL

WINNING THE TRIPLE CROWN

Graham Hill is the only racing driver in history to have won the legendary so-called 'Triple Crown' of motor racing: the F1 Drivers' Championship, the Indy 500 (which he entered in 1966-1968 and won at his first attempt), and Le Mans (left), which he competed in on ten occasions and won in 1972 with Frenchman Henri Pescarolo.

Graham Hill didn't start a race of any kind until he was 25, when he made his F3 debut in a Cooper 500 in 1954. Although he joined Lotus soon after, it was initially as a mechanic, the team weren't really considering him as driver material. But Hill was. He quickly talked his way into a car and made his F1 debut at Monaco in 1958 but had to retire with mechanical failure. An inauspicious start for a man who came to be known as 'Mr Monaco' in tribute to his then-record five wins at the circuit. Hill went on to start a then-record 176 Grands Prix, winning world titles in 1962 and 1968. He set up his own team, Embassy Hill, in 1973, but two years later Hill, his protégé Tony Brise, and five team executives were killed in an air crash (Hill was piloting). Embassy Hill were shut down in the wake of the tragedy.

BIO

DATE OF BIRTH: 15 February 1929
BIRTHPLACE: Hampstead, England
NATIONALITY: British
YEARS ACTIVE: 1958-1975
TEAMS: Lotus (1958-59), BRM (1960-66), Lotus (1967-69), Walker (1970), Brabham (1971-72), Hill (1973-75)
FIRST ENTRY: 1958 Monaco Grand Prix

F1 CAREER

2 F1 Championship wins (1962, 1968)
14 wins
36 podiums
13 pole positions

STATS & RECORDS

5 – wins at the Monaco Grand Prix
24 – the age at which he passed his driving test
19 – number of F1 races before gaining his first point

IMAGES: ADOBE STOCK, GETTY

 **FORMULA 1 ALL-STARS**

The **SMILING ASSASSIN** who looks like he wouldn't harm a fly, but under the surface is a **RUTHLESS TEAMMATE-CRUSHER**

GEORGE RUSSELL

When Formula 1 drivers get to the end of their career there are many metrics by which they're judged: world titles, race wins, pole positions and more. But another measure of ability is how you compete against your teammates. This is somewhere that George Russell shines. After impressing in GP3 and Formula 2, he made his debut with Williams in 2019. He outqualified the experienced Robert Kubica in every race, although he failed to score a point. That record earned him a one-off race for Mercedes in 2020 with Lewis Hamilton out with Covid-19, before a historic second in a rain-aborted Belgian Grand Prix. He clearly impressed as Mercedes snapped him up to replace Valtteri Bottas to complete an all-British pairing with Hamilton. He settled instantly, finishing ahead of his illustrious teammate in 2022 and 2024, winning three races. With the seven-time champ off to Ferrari, Russell now steps up as undisputed team leader, which should let us see what he's really made of.

FAST FACT
Russell won the GP3 Series in 2017 and Formula 2 in 2018.

63
GEORGE RUSSELL

BIO
DATE OF BIRTH: 15 February 1998
BIRTHPLACE: King's Lynn, England
NATIONALITY: British
YEARS ACTIVE: 2019-present
TEAMS: Williams (2019-21), Mercedes (2022-present)
FIRST ENTRY: 2019 Australian Grand Prix

F1 CAREER
0 F1 Championships
3 wins
15 podiums
5 pole positions

STATS & RECORDS
37 – races before first points

0.000s – smallest gap between 1st and 2nd in qualifying (Russell & Verstappen at 2024 Canadian GP)

7 – joint most pit stops in a race (2023 Dutch GP)

IMAGES: ADOBE STOCK, GETTY

FORMULA 1 ALL-STARS

DID YOU KNOW?
He is nicknamed 'Mr Saturday' due to impressive performances in qualifying.

SÃO PAULO SMILES

>>> With just two races left of the 2022 season, Mercedes hadn't taken a chequered flag. However, in São Paulo the two Silver Arrows found themselves at the front. Lewis Hamilton was trying to avoid the first winless season in his career, Russell a first-ever victory. And it was the younger man who triumphed, finishing 1.5 seconds clear for a memorable victory.

BELGIUM JOY

>>> Williams hadn't stood on the podium since 2017, but all that changed in odd circumstances in Belgium 2021. Russell put in a phenomenal qualifying performance to put himself second on the grid for Sunday. However, it poured with rain all day, forcing a lengthy delay before finally the cars completed three laps behind the safety car. Half-points were awarded and Russell took the champagne for the first time.

GEORGE RUSSELL

›››Belgium hasn't always been so kind to Russell. He thought he had pulled off a masterclass at Spa in 2024, running a one-stop strategy and holding off a charging Hamilton to take the flag. However, devastatingly, his car was found to be just under the weight limit. He was disqualified, plummeting from the high of a historic win to the low of a DQ and no points.

HEARTBREAK AT SPA

> "He took the promotion in his stride, qualifying second behind Valtteri Bottas"

SAKHIR FRUSTRATION

›››At Sakhir 2020 Russell, part of the junior Mercedes driver programme, got the call-up to sub in for Hamilton, who had Covid-19. He took the promotion in his stride, qualifying second behind Valtteri Bottas. He took the lead from the start, a botched pit stop pushed him back, he battled back up to second, but a late puncture ended his hopes. He had four pit stops in all, eventually finishing ninth.

FORMULA 1 ALL-STARS

TOP 10 F1 RACES

1995 European Grand Prix
NÜRBURGRING

>>> A damp track saw Jean Alesi take the lead in his Ferrari, but Benetton's Michael Schumacher took advantage of a lighter fuel load and fresh tyres after his last stop and spent the last 15 laps relentlessly cutting into Alesi's 24-second margin. Schumacher took the lead with two laps to go to take the chequered flag and all but secure the Drivers' Championship.

1988 Japanese Grand Prix
SUZUKA

>>> Suzuka was the venue of three consecutive title deciders between Alain Prost and Ayrton Senna, and this race showcased the drivers at their best. Senna dropped from pole position to 14th after stalling on the grid, but he drove the rest of the race like a man possessed. He overtook Prost for the lead on lap 27 and held it to the end for his first Drivers' Championship.

2008 Brazilian Grand Prix
INTERLAGOS

>>> Home favourite Felipe Massa thought he'd done enough to win the Drivers' Championship when he crossed the line in first place, but the race wasn't over yet. Title rival Lewis Hamilton was in sixth, but needed to finish fifth to leapfrog Massa in the standings. Hamilton overtook Timo Glock on the last corner to seal his first championship win and leave the Brazilian fans in stunned silence.

1971 Italian Grand Prix
MONZA

>>> The closest finish of all time saw the first five cars cross the line within six-tenths of a second of each other. Peter Gethin went from fourth to first on the last lap to claim his only F1 win by 0.01 seconds from Ronnie Peterson, and he set an average speed record of 150.754mph (242.615kph) that lasted until 2003.

2021 Abu Dhabi Grand Prix
YAS MARINA

>>> Lewis Hamilton looked on course to win a record eighth Drivers' Championship when he led the race with five laps to go. Most expected the race to end under the safety car after Nicholas Latifi ran off the track, but the race director's unexpected decision to allow a final lap of racing allowed Max Verstappen to overtake Hamilton and win the title in controversial circumstances.

TOP 10 F1 RACES

There have been **MORE THAN 1,000 F1 RACES** since the championship began – these classics make it into **THE TOP 1%**

1986 Australian Grand Prix
ADELAIDE

>>> Nigel Mansell was locked in a battle for the Drivers' Championship with teammate Nelson Piquet and Alain Prost, but Mansell pushed too hard and suffered a dramatic tyre blowout. That left Piquet to fight it out with Prost, but Prost did enough to hold off the Brazilian's late charge and take the title by four seconds.

2011 Canadian Grand Prix
CIRCUIT GILLES VILLENEUVE

>>> Rain dampened the mood in Montreal, but Jenson Button didn't mind one bit. He survived two prangs with other cars, served a drive-through penalty, and at one stage was in last place. However, he took advantage of six safety car deployments to work his way back up, overtaking race leader Vettel on the last lap for a legendary victory.

1996 Monaco Grand Prix
MONACO

>>> When it rains in Monaco, there's little leeway if things go wrong. 21 cars started the 1996 race, but by the time the race had run its full distance, only three drivers were left. Olivier Panis recorded a rare win for Ligier, while David Coulthard and Johnny Herbert took their places on the podium simply because they managed to cross the line.

1964 Mexican Grand Prix
MAGDELANA MIXHUCA

>>> A three-way fight for the Drivers' Championship went down to the last lap of the last race. Graham Hill was ruled out of contention when he spun into a barrier. That left Jim Clark on course for the title until his engine seized on the last lap. Ferrari bosses frantically signalled for John Surtees to pass his teammate Lorenzo Bandini, giving him enough points to take the World Drivers' Championship.

2012 Brazilian Grand Prix
INTERLAGOS

>>> With a then-record 147 overtakes, the last race of 2012 saw several lead changes in both the race and the Drivers' Championship. It finished with Jenson Button on the top step of the podium and Sebastian Vettel as the Drivers' Champion for the third year in a row, despite Vettel dropping to last place on the opening lap after a tangle with Bruno Senna.

IMAGES: ADOBE STOCK, ALAMY, GETTY

FORMULA 1 ALL-STARS

PASSIONATE, AGGRESSIVE and **INSTINCTIVE,** Senna was in many ways the **ULTIMATE DRIVER** in the ultimate driving sport

AYRTON SENNA

FAST FACT
Senna won six races in three seasons with Lotus before his move to McLaren.

27 AYRTON SENNA

Senna driving the McLaren-Honda MP4/5B at the Grand Prix of France in 1990

Senna was a driver of immense natural talent. Frank Williams, team principal at the Williams Racing team, once described him as "the best piece of equipment... you could put in the machine".

A deeply religious man, his driving often seemed to be inspired. He talked of entering a "different dimension" when at the wheel, and no driver before or since has matched his racing instinct and dashing style. At times even he failed to understand exactly how he was managing to drive so fast – his opponents could only wonder as well.

Some believed he had a little too much confidence when pushing himself and his machine to the limit. His teammate and great rival, Alain Prost, commented, "Ayrton has a small problem. He thinks that he can't kill himself because he believes in God…"

It was to prove a sadly prophetic statement when Senna died after a crash in Italy in 1994.

BIO

DATE OF BIRTH: 21 March 1960
BIRTHPLACE: São Paulo, Brazil
NATIONALITY: Brazilian
YEARS ACTIVE: 1984-94
TEAMS: Toleman (1984), Lotus (1985-87), McLaren (1988-93), Williams (1994)
FIRST ENTRY: 1984 Brazilian Grand Prix

F1 CAREER

3 F1 Championships (1988, 1990, 1991)
41 wins
80 podiums
65 pole positions

STATS & RECORDS

8 – most consecutive pole positions

100% – highest percentage front row starts in a season (1989)

5 – most consecutive wins at the same GP (Monaco)

IMAGES: ADOBE STOCK, GETTY

FORMULA 1 ALL-STARS

DID YOU KNOW?
Senna won 13 out of 16 pole positions during the 1988 season.

KARTING KID

›› Senna's love of racing was triggered when his father gave him a go-kart at the age of four, and he was soon watching Grands Prix on television, dreaming of one day being on the starting grid himself. He won the South American Karting Championship in 1977 and often said it was his favourite form of racing, returning to it for fun as late as 1993.

THE KING OF MONACO

›› Senna excelled on the narrow street circuit at Monaco, especially in the wet. In only his sixth F1 race, driving for the uncompetitive Tuleman-Hart team, he almost pulled off a stunning win as he was chasing down Alain Prost when the race was abandoned due to heavy rain. He would later win five Monaco Grands Prix in a row from 1989 to 1993.

IMAGES: ADOBE STOCK, GETTY

BEST OF ENEMIES

>>> Senna's rivalry with Prost was legendary. After nearly beating the Frenchman in his sixth race, they became the fiercest of competitors. Teammates at McLaren-Honda in 1988, they won 15 of 16 races between them, with Senna grabbing his first Drivers' Championship. Prost drove Senna off the track at Suzuka in 1989, winning the title in the process, and Senna took Prost out at the same track the following year to win his second championship.

THE DEATH THAT CHANGED F1

>>> Following the tragic death of Senna at Imola in 1994, F1 entered a period of sustained safety enhancements. Many of the innovations brought in were direct consequences of Senna's crash. The most visible modification in this ongoing drive to make the sport as safe as possible was the addition of the 'halo' in 2010, which protects the driver's head from the kind of impact that took Senna's life.

FORMULA 1 ALL-STARS

The nearly man of Formula 1 who **ROSE TO THE TOP** *of the mountain and chose to* **GO OUT ON A HIGH**

NICO ROSBERG

Nico Rosberg entered Formula 1 with a lot of pressure, as the son of 1982 World Champion Keke. His success in Formula BMW earned him a drive at his father's team, Williams. He impressed, earning two podiums in his third season. Then came the dream for any German, a seat at Mercedes alongside legend Michael Schumacher. Rosberg lived the dream, outqualifying and outracing the seven-time champ. Schumacher's retirement brought Lewis Hamilton to the team – sparking the ultimate teammate rivalry. New engine regulations in 2014 helped the pair dominate and, despite Rosberg's long-time lead, Hamilton took the title. The following season was less close due to a series of Rosberg errors. However, in 2016 Rosberg returned with a laser focus. It went down to the final race and the German took an emotional title. Five days later he dramatically retired, citing the sacrifice of his family, the pressure and hard work in achieving his dream. To win a title is incredible, to do it after an epic battle with your teammate is historic, to retire less than a week later is the ultimate mic drop.

FAST FACT
Nico, like his father Keke, confirmed his only World Championship in the final race of the season.

6
NICO ROSBERG

WHEN TEAM MATES COLLIDE

Rosberg and Hamilton's rivalry was epic. Hamilton refused to move over for Rosberg in Hungary 2014, then Rosberg hit Hamilton in Belgium. A Rosberg error at USA 2015 handed Hamilton the title. The champ threw Rosberg his 2nd place cap and Rosberg hurled it back. Then in Spain 2016, the pair collided on the opening lap, retiring them both. Then in Abu Dhabi, Hamilton tried to back Rosberg into traffic to overhaul his lead. A controversial end to a feisty partnership.

BIO

DATE OF BIRTH: 27 June 1985
BIRTHPLACE: Wiesbaden, Germany
NATIONALITY: German
YEARS ACTIVE: 2006-16
TEAMS: Williams (2006-09), Mercedes (2010-16)
FIRST ENTRY: 2006 Bahrain Grand Prix

F1 CAREER

1 F1 Championships (2016)
23 wins
57 podiums
30 pole positions

STATS & RECORDS

30 – most pole positions before becoming World Champion

31 – most 1-2 finishes (with Lewis Hamilton)

4 – consecutive wins at start of 2016 season

IMAGES: ADOBE STOCK, GETTY

FORMULA 1 ALL-STARS

The **ONLY ITALIAN TO BECOME WORLD CHAMPION**, Ascari would have **WON MORE** but for his untimely death

ALBERTO ASCARI

Like a lot of drivers in the early years of the Formula 1 World Championship, Italian Alberto Ascari was known for his calm and precise driving style. He could drive fast, but he much preferred to get out in front of the field and lead them all the way home – a sensible approach in the days when playing catch-up or attempting to overtake your rivals could easily end in disaster, even tragedy. Ascari was reputedly very difficult to get past. His move to Lancia in 1954 – after salary disputes with Ferrari – was reckoned to be a bad one; the Lancia was quick but unreliable, though it's worth noting that he did win the Mille Miglia that year in a Lancia sportscar. The 1955 season started well, with the Lancia beating the previously all-conquering Mercedes in non-championship races. But in testing a Ferrari 750 sportscar at Monza, Ascari was tragically killed.

FAST FACT
When he was nearly seven, Ascari's father was killed in an accident during the 1925 French Grand Prix.

11
ALBERTO ASCARI

THE DEATH OF ASCARI

At the 1955 Monaco Grand Prix, Ascari was leading the race when he misjudged a chicane and drove into the harbour. Remarkably, although his car sank, Ascari walked away with nothing more than a broken nose. Perhaps the notoriously superstitious Italian felt luck was on his side, but just four days later at Monza he was trying a few laps of practice in a Ferrari sportscar when it flipped and somersaulted. Ascari was thrown from the car and died shortly after.

BIO

DATE OF BIRTH: 13 July 1918
BIRTHPLACE: Milan, Italy
NATIONALITY: Italian
YEARS ACTIVE: 1950-55
TEAMS: Ferrari (1950-53), Maserati (1954), Lancia (1954-55)
FIRST ENTRY: 1950 Monaco Grand Prix

F1 CAREER

2 F1 Championship wins (1952, 1953)
13 wins
17 podiums
14 pole positions

STATS & RECORDS

3 – most Grand Slams in a season

0 – F1 races lost between June 1952 and June 1953

40.63% – wins to starts ratio

IMAGES: ADOBE STOCK, GETTY

FORMULA 1 ALL-STARS

Emerging as one of **F1'S MOST EXCITING TALENTS**, Lando Norris is widely tipped to be a **FUTURE WORLD CHAMPION**

LANDO NORRIS

Lando Norris's childhood passion for karting culminated in a world championship title by the age of 14, followed by successes in junior driving categories, including triumphs in MSA Formula, Formula Renault, and FIA Formula 3. In 2019, still a teenager, Norris graduated to Formula 1 with McLaren, a team he has remained loyal to throughout his top-flight career.

In his rookie season, Norris impressed with standout performances, frequently outqualifying teammate Carlos Sainz and consistently scoring points, and claimed his maiden podium in 2020. Norris's breakthrough came in 2024, with four race wins and a fierce challenge for Max Verstappen's title, and, along with teammate Oscar Piastri, he helped McLaren secure their first Constructors' Championship since 1998.

Off the track, Norris's cheeky charm has made him a firm fan favourite. Reflecting his Belgian heritage, he speaks some Flemish Dutch, showcases artistic flair, and is an entrepreneur, founding Quadrant, a brand combining his passions for gaming, racing, content and apparel.

FAST FACT
Lando's favourite circuit to drive is Great Britain's Silverstone.

4 LANDO NORRIS

BIO

DATE OF BIRTH: 13 November 1999
BIRTHPLACE: Bristol, England
NATIONALITY: British
YEARS ACTIVE: 2019-present
TEAMS: McLaren (2019-present)
FIRST ENTRY: 2019 Australian Grand Prix

F1 CAREER

0 F1 Championships
4 wins
26 podiums
9 pole positions

STATS & RECORDS

7.87 – average points per race
12 – fastest laps
79.69% – percentage of points-scoring races

IMAGES: ADOBE STOCK, GETTY

FORMULA 1 ALL-STARS

DID YOU KNOW?
He became McLaren's youngest ever F1 driver at 19 years old.

FIRST F1 PODIUM

>>> In a thrilling season opener to the 2020 season following a break for the pandemic, Norris claimed his maiden F1 podium at the Austrian Grand Prix, finishing third behind Valtteri Bottas and Charles Leclerc. He also set the fastest lap on the final lap of the race, and at 20 became the youngest British driver to score a podium.

BREAKTHROUGH WIN

>>> Securing his first ever F1 race victory at the 2024 Miami Grand Prix, Norris finally had the long-awaited triumph he needed, marking the beginning of his most successful season and helping to establish him as a serious title contender.

IMAGES: ADOBE STOCK, GETTY

LANDO NORRIS

2024 CONSTRUCTORS' CHAMPIONSHIP

>>> Playing a more than pivotal role in helping McLaren secure their first Constructors' Championship since 1998, Norris's consistent performances and four race wins helped to bring Red Bull's dominance to an end.

POLE POSITION TO HEARTBREAK

>>> In Sochi at the 2021 Russian Grand Prix, Norris earned his first career pole position and led much of the race. But hope turned to despair as weather conditions changed and a late-race tyre gamble failed to pay off, dashing his hopes of a podium as he aquaplaned out of contention and into 7th place.

FORMULA 1 ALL-STARS

Although BORN INTO WEALTH, Niki Lauda had to PAY HIS OWN WAY into racing, but it ALMOST COST HIM HIS LIFE…

NIKI LAUDA

Born into a prestigious Austrian banking dynasty in 1949, Niki Lauda defied his family's wishes to pursue his motor racing dream, funding early opportunities through bank loans. But the gamble paid off, and in 1971 he made his F1 debut. Despite some early challenges, Lauda's talent secured him a Ferrari seat in 1974, leading to his first World Championship in 1975. A horrific crash at the 1976 German Grand Prix almost claimed his life, yet, permanently disfigured by the blazing inferno, he miraculously returned just weeks later. Lauda went on to claim two more titles (1977 and 1984) before retiring in 1985. Beyond racing, he built a successful aviation career and mentored future F1 legends, including Lewis Hamilton. Known for his resilience and calculated driving, he earned the nickname 'The Computer', and when he passed away in 2019, aged 70, he left behind an indelible legacy in motorsport.

FAST FACT
In 1982, Niki Lauda led a successful drivers' strike opposing restrictive contract clauses.

11
NIKI LAUDA

DOWN BUT NOT OUT

A week before the German Grand Prix at the Nürburgring, Lauda urged his fellow competitors to boycott the race due to severe safety concerns, but due to a lack of support the race went ahead. On the second lap, Lauda's car veered into a wall at full speed, burst into flames, and was struck by two oncoming cars. Miraculously, he survived despite third-degree burns, broken bones, and lung damage, and only missed two races before returning just five and a half weeks later.

BIO

DATE OF BIRTH: 22 February 1949
BIRTHPLACE: Vienna, Austria
NATIONALITY: Austrian
YEARS ACTIVE: 1971-79, 1982-85
TEAMS: March (1971-72), BRM (1973), Ferrari (1974-77), Brabham (1978-79), McLaren (1982-85)
FIRST ENTRY: 1971 Austrian Grand Prix

F1 CAREER

3 F1 Championships (1975, 1977, 1984)
25 wins
54 podiums
24 pole positions

STATS & RECORDS

7 YEARS – longest gap between successive titles (1977 and 1984)

0 – number of pole positions in the 1984 title-winning season

0.5 – number of points he won the 1984 title by (ahead of Alain Prost)

IMAGES: ADOBE STOCK, GETTY

FORMULA 1 ALL-STARS

The OUTSPOKEN CANADIAN whose entry to the F1 scene CAME WITH A BANG

JACQUES VILLENEUVE

Although Villeneuve was already an IndyCar champion and Indianapolis 500 winner at the age of 24, some critics claimed that he was only given an F1 seat by Williams in 1996 thanks to his famous surname. However, Villeneuve – the son of former Ferrari legend Gilles – quickly repaid his new team. He finished second in the Drivers' Championship in his debut season, pushing teammate Damon Hill all the way to the final race and only capitulating when a wheel came off his car. The following year, Villeneuve stepped into the senior seat at Williams and again the title went down to the last race of the season. This time it was Villeneuve who finished while his rival Michael Schumacher didn't, giving Villeneuve his first and only F1 Championship. Although Villeneuve bounced around the grid in his later years in Formula 1, it's his action-packed first two seasons that he'll always be remembered for.

FAST FACT
Villeneuve is the only Canadian to have won the World Drivers' Championship.

JACQUES VILLENEUVE

17

TAKING THE TITLE

Going into the last race of the 1997 season, Villeneuve needed to finish ahead of Michael Schumacher to take the title. On lap 48, he attempted the title-winning move, but Schumacher was having none of it and the two cars collided. Villeneuve dropped to third, but since Schumacher's self-inflicted damage caused him to retire, it was enough for Villeneuve to claim the championship.

BIO

DATE OF BIRTH: 9 April 1971
BIRTHPLACE: Saint-Jean-sur-Richelieu, Canada
NATIONALITY: Canadian
YEARS ACTIVE: 1996-2006
TEAMS: Williams (1996-98), BAR (1999-2003), Renault (2004), Sauber (2005-06)
FIRST ENTRY: 1996 Australian Grand Prix

F1 CAREER

1 F1 Championship (1997)
11 wins
23 podiums
13 pole positions

STATS & RECORDS

4 – joint-most wins in debut season
2nd – joint-highest finish in debut season
2 – joint-fewest seasons before first title

IMAGES: ADOBE STOCK, GETTY

FORMULA 1 ALL-STARS

With MORE LAPS AND MORE MILES than any other driver, Alonso has a reputation for **CONSISTENCY, FOCUS and AGGRESSION**

FERNANDO ALONSO

No driver has put in more time than Fernando Alonso – over 21 (and counting) dramatic seasons, he has travelled further than any other F1 driver in history. And his career includes two seasons when he was retired, so he could have gone even further.

Like most great drivers, Alonso took to the sport from an early age, but not many can say they got their first drive in an F1 car as part of a tournament prize. The young Spaniard quickly progressed after getting his chance, becoming a test driver for Renault in 2002, and in just his fourth season of racing he won the first of two consecutive Drivers' Championships.

An aggressive driver, Alonso has been compared to the great Ayrton Senna in his ability to know where a track offers the best grip. His remarkable skill in knowing exactly how late he can leave braking allows him to extract maximum pace from his car.

FAST FACT
Fernando's first go-kart was actually built for his sister, Lorena, but she wasn't interested.

14
FERNANDO ALONSO

BIO

DATE OF BIRTH: 29 July 1981
BIRTHPLACE: Oviedo, Spain
NATIONALITY: Spanish
YEARS ACTIVE: 2001-present
TEAMS: Minardi (2001), Renault (2003-06), McLaren (2007), Renault (2008-09), Ferrari (2010-2014), McLaren (2015-18), Alpine (2021-22), Aston Martin (2023-present)
FIRST ENTRY: 2001 Australian Grand Prix

F1 CAREER

2 F1 Championships (2005, 2006)
32 wins
106 podiums
22 pole positions

STATS & RECORDS

404 – most race entries
401 – most total starts
324 – most career race finishes

FORMULA 1 ALL-STARS

DID YOU KNOW?
Alonso has driven the most Grand Prix laps (21,827 and counting) of any F1 driver.

THE ULTIMATE PRIZE

>>> Alonso's success in the 1999 Euro Open by Nissan, at the age of 17, brought a priceless reward – a chance to drive a Minardi F1 car. He impressed the team so much they gave him a seat in their F3000 team for the 2000 season and a position as a test driver for their F1 outfit. The next year, he started his first race for Minardi, in Australia.

RECORD BREAKER

>>> In 2005, Alonso became the youngest (at the time) driver to win a Drivers' Championship, beating the previous record held by Emerson Fittipaldi. The triumph came after a brilliant season that saw him amass 133 points from 15 podium finishes, including seven victories, to hold off a stiff challenge from main rival Kimi Räikkönen.

IMAGES: ADOBE STOCK, GETTY

MR VERSATILE

>>> Alonso is one of only five F1 Champions to have also won the gruelling 24-hour endurance race at Le Mans. Driving for Toyota Gazoo Racing, he won in both 2018 and 2019, both times with co-drivers Sébastien Buemi and Kazuki Nakajima. The 2018 victory was the first for Toyota, having entered 47 cars in previous races.

> "Alonso is one of only five F1 Champions to have also won… at Le Mans"

THE COMEBACK KID

>>> Alonso retired from F1 at the end of the 2018 season – he finished 11th in the Drivers' Championship, scoring 50 points, but had become disillusioned with the McLaren team. He returned to the sport with Alpine (the new incarnation of the Renault F1 team) in 2021, seeing it as a chance to repay the team that brought him his two Drivers' Championships.

FORMULA 1 ALL-STARS

TOP 10 F1 CIRCUITS

Uncover some of the **MOST ICONIC RACE TRACKS** in Formula 1 history

MONACO

>>> The Monaco Grand Prix isn't just a race – it's the most famous event on the Formula 1 calendar. The tight street circuit through Monte Carlo doesn't result in much overtaking, but it's the place where drivers most want to stand on the top step of the podium, and it's the weekend when race fans mingle with hundreds of A-list celebrities.

CIRCUIT GILLES VILLENEUVE

>>> Canada's F1 circuit is a tough track to handle, and even the best sometimes get it wrong. Four drivers, three of whom were former champions, crashed there coming out of the final chicane in 1999, giving birth to a new nickname: 'the Wall of Champions'. Circuit Gilles Villeneuve has also played host to some great races, including Jenson Button's last-gasp win in 2011.

NÜRBURGRING

>>> The original Nürburgring was the longest F1 track at more than 13 miles (21 kilometres) long with a mind-boggling 154 corners. It was surrounded by forest and almost impossible to monitor the progress of drivers. Thankfully, the F1 track was shortened to a more manageable three-mile (4.8-kilometre) loop in 1984 and it's since played host to several great races.

SUZUKA

>>> Suzuka's elongated shape is the only figure-of-eight track on the F1 calendar, with cars roaring overhead thanks to an overpass halfway around each lap. It was added to the end of the race schedule in 1987 and immediately became a fan favourite thanks to legendary battles between Ayrton Senna and Alain Prost.

INTERLAGOS

>>> A hilly circuit squeezed between two man-made lakes that supply São Paulo's drinking water, Interlagos has a counterclockwise layout which places stress on both drivers and cars. The Brazilian Grand Prix has closed out the season several times, so Interlagos has played host to several significant moments in F1 history, including Lewis Hamilton's last-lap championship-winning overtake in 2008.

A RACING GOD
Ayrton Senna is widely considered to be one of the best F1 drivers ever, but sadly he was taken in his prime after a crash in 1994
IMAGE: MIKE HEWITT / GETTY

EL MATADOR
Fernando Alonso has driven more laps and more miles than any other F1 driver, winning two Drivers' Championships in the process

IMAGE: MARK THOMPSON / GETTY

MR SATURDAY
While he's yet to win a title, George Russell will be looking to step out of the departing Lewis Hamilton's shadow and establish himself as the No.1 driver at Mercedes

BILLION DOLLAR MAN
Lewis Hamilton will be aiming for an unprecedented eighth Drivers' Championship after moving to the iconic Ferrari team in 2025

IMAGE BRYN LENNON / GETTY

MCLAREN'S MAIN MAN
Lando Norris has become a firm fan favourite and will be hoping to go one better than his second-place Drivers' Championship finish in 2024

THE WIZARD OF AUS
Alongside teammate Lando Norris, Oscar Piastri helped McLaren to their first Constructors' title in over 25 years in the 2024 F1 season

PRINCE OF MONACO
Charles Leclerc will be hoping to bring the glory days back to Ferrari alongside new teammate Lewis Hamilton

THE FLYING DUTCHMAN
Verstappen has dominated Formula 1 in recent years, winning four Drivers' Championships in a row between 2021 and 2024

TOP 10 F1 CIRCUITS

SILVERSTONE
>>> In 1948, the British Racing Drivers' Club remodelled a disused World War II airfield and transformed it into a super-fast racing circuit. Just two years later, Silverstone became the venue for the first F1 World Championship race. Although the track and its facilities are almost unrecognisable from that inaugural race, Silverstone retains a particular allure for its historical significance.

MARINA BAY
>>> The Singapore Grand Prix is always spectacular given that racing takes place on the streets of Marina Bay at night. Drivers dislike the bumpy circuit, but they can't deny that it takes them on a spectacular tour of Singapore's sights, including the Fullerton Hotel, Anderson Bridge and the iconic Singapore Flyer ferris wheel.

MONZA
>>> The Italian Grand Prix guarantees a passionate crowd since it's the home race for the Ferrari faithful, but the historic Monza circuit adds to the spectacle too. The third-oldest race track in the world is fast, with long straights and high-speed corners. No track has hosted more F1 races than Monza, and it seems set to stay on the calendar for years to come.

SPA-FRANCORCHAMPS
>>> Belgium's most famous racing circuit, Circuit de Spa-Francorchamps is the kind of track that separates the champions from the also-rans. It's best known for the Eau Rouge and Raidillon combination, where drivers race downhill before launching up a steep uphill with a series of corners. Only the best drivers can make it stick at speed.

RED BULL RING
>>> Originally known as the Österreichring, then remodelled as the A1 Ring, this mountainous circuit in southeast Austria was adapted again and reopened in 2011 as the Red Bull Ring. The various iterations have seen some classic races, including a bad-tempered clash between teammates Lewis Hamilton and Nico Rosberg in 2016 and a masterclass by Alain Prost in 1983.

IMAGES: ADOBE STOCK, GETTY

FORMULA 1 ALL-STARS

Few **DRIVERS ARE AS CONTROVERSIAL** as the flying Dutchman, who blends **SUPREME COURAGE** with a fierce determination to win

MAX VERSTAPPEN

Some drivers arrive on the scene like a thunderclap, demanding attention and forcing established drivers to look nervously over their shoulders. Max Verstappen was that kind of driver. From the moment he first stepped into an F1 car, he has attracted attention and controversy.

His driving style, based on race experience rather than analysis of data, was extremely fast and very aggressive. Some complained that he was sure to cause a major accident at some point if he didn't calm down, but although he has gained experience, he continues to drive on the edge and he is still taking frequent penalties for reckless driving.

Despite this, his first Drivers' Championship, in 2021, opened the door on an era of dominance that is still rumbling on, and until a driver emerges with the skill, the car and the courage to take him on, he will remain at the very top of the sport.

FAST FACT
Max's girlfriend is Kelly Piquet, daughter of F1 legend Nelson Piquet.

MAX VERSTAPPEN 1

Verstappen is greeted by F1 legend Jackie Stewart prior to the 2024 Grand Prix of Abu Dhabi

BIO

DATE OF BIRTH: 30 September 1997
BIRTHPLACE: Hasselt, Belgium
NATIONALITY: Dutch-Belgian
YEARS ACTIVE: 2015-present
TEAMS: Toro Rosso (2015-16), Red Bull (2016-present)
FIRST ENTRY: 2015 Australian Grand Prix

F1 CAREER

4 F1 Championships (2021, 2022, 2023, 2024)
63 wins
112 podiums
40 pole positions

STATS & RECORDS

17 YEARS, 166 DAYS – youngest driver to start a Grand Prix
19 – most wins in a season
86.36% – highest percentage of wins in a season

IMAGES: ADOBE STOCK, GETTY

FORMULA 1 ALL-STARS

DID YOU KNOW?
Verstappen's legion of Dutch supporters is known as the 'Orange Army'.

GOING DUTCH

>>> Max holds dual citizenship, having been born in Belgium to Belgian and Dutch parents. He has wavered in his opinion about this, sometimes claiming to feel more Dutch (he chose to race under the Dutch flag) and to have only used Belgium as a place to sleep, but now he admits to being 'half-half'.

THE YOUNG PRETENDER

>>> Toro Rosso were planning to give Verstappen a car for the 2015 season, so they gave him a little experience the year before. At just 17 years and three days old, Max became the youngest driver ever to take part in a Grand Prix weekend when he took a practice session prior to the 2014 Japanese Grand Prix.

IMAGES: ADOBE STOCK, GETTY

MAX VERSTAPPEN

FIRST IMPRESSIONS

>>> Verstappen very quickly gained a reputation as an aggressive and headstrong young driver. Some expressed concern that he was a little too aggressive, and he was involved in numerous shunts – but at the end of his first season, in 2015, he was voted Rookie of the Year and Personality of the Year, while his overtaking of Felipe Nasr at the Belgian Grand Prix was voted Action of the Year.

LAST GASP VICTORY

>>> Verstappen's first Drivers' Championship came in controversial circumstances. Tied with Lewis Hamilton at the top of the table, the last race saw the Englishman lead from the first corner to the finish... almost. An accident at the end of the race brought out a safety car and Verstappen took the opportunity to change tyres. In a desperate last lap, he then overtook Hamilton to claim the title.

FORMULA 1 ALL-STARS

James 'THE SHUNT' Hunt lived a FAST AND FURIOUS playboy lifestyle – and we loved him for it

JAMES HUNT

Despite his nickname, the evidence doesn't really support the idea that Hunt had more crashes than other drivers, except in his early days. He was certainly quick, and sometimes reckless, but never dangerous. Niki Lauda once said of him: "You could drive next to him – two centimetres, wheel-by-wheel, for 300 kilometres or more – and nothing would happen." The truth was that the cars weren't terribly reliable in the 1970s, and Hunt's dynamic racing style and serious bursts of speed put them under greater pressure than some other drivers. It is easy to forget that Hunt only raced seven seasons in F1, and arguably had a competitive car for just two of them. He took his chance, though, snatching his sole Drivers' Championship in 1976 from his great friend Lauda. Against expectation, Hunt made a new career out of race-day commentary where he proved to be the perfect outspoken foil to Murray Walker as F1 exploded onto TV.

FAST FACT
His fee for an exhibition race to open the new Nürburgring circuit in 1984 was a Triumph Bonneville motorbike.

11 JAMES HUNT

BIO

DATE OF BIRTH: 29 August 1947
BIRTHPLACE: Belmont, England
NATIONALITY: British
YEARS ACTIVE: 1973-79
TEAMS: Hesketh (1973-75), McLaren (1976-78), Wolf (1979)
FIRST ENTRY: 1973 Monaco Grand Prix

F1 CAREER

1 F1 Championships (1976)
10 wins
23 podiums
14 pole positions

STATS & RECORDS

1 – number of points by which he won the 1976 Drivers' Championship

£2.6m – the amount he was offered by Bernie Ecclestone of Brabham to make a comeback in 1982

8 – number of fastest laps in his F1 career

FRIENDS BEFORE FOES

In an era when rivalries stayed on the track, Hunt and Niki Lauda were genuine friends. They had travelled around Europe together in their Formula 3 days, and Lauda occasionally stayed with Hunt. Ronnie Peterson was another close friend (left, rear behind Hunt), although the Swede was naturally quieter than the larger-than-life Hunt. Hunt was devastated by Peterson's death in 1978, which undoubtedly played a large part in his decision to quit a year later.

IMAGES: ADOBE STOCK, GETTY

FORMULA 1 ALL-STARS

FAST FACT
Ricciardo was awarded a Member of the Order of Australia in the 2022 Australia Day Honours.

With **MAVERICK-STYLE RACING** and **CAPTIVATING CHARM**, the self-proclaimed **'HONEY BADGER'** remains one of the sport's most **ICONIC PERSONALITIES**

DANIEL RICCIARDO

DANIEL RICCIARDO

MAKING HISTORY AT MONZA

One of Ricciardo's most celebrated races came at the 2021 Monza Grand Prix, where he seized the lead by overtaking Max Verstappen at the start and held it for 21 laps before pitting. A dramatic collision between Verstappen and Lewis Hamilton took both title contenders out of contention, allowing Ricciardo to capitalise and secure his first victory since 2018. The win also marked McLaren's first since 2012, with teammate Lando Norris finishing second to deliver a historic one-two finish – the team's first since 2010.

One thing Daniel Ricciardo has in spades is charisma – his magnetic personality, infectious humour, and trademark grin have made him a beloved fan favourite. While he may not have cemented his legacy as one of F1's all-time greats, his fearless overtakes and unwavering tenacity firmly established him as the one and only 'Honey Badger'.

Starting as a test driver for Scuderia Toro Rocco in 2011, Ricciardo debuted at the British Grand Prix with HRT before securing a Toro Rosso seat in 2012. His talent caught Red Bull Racing's attention, leading to a promotion in 2014, where he claimed three wins and eight podiums.

Seeking fresh challenges, Ricciardo moved to Renault in 2019, delivering podiums that revitalised the team. A switch to McLaren in 2021 brought a stunning Monza victory, their first win since 2012. However, after a challenging 2022 season, Ricciardo returned to Red Bull as a reserve driver in 2023, before moving to AlphaTauri (later renamed RB) on loan until he was replaced mid-2024 by Liam Lawson.

BIO

DATE OF BIRTH: 1 July 1989
BIRTHPLACE: Perth, Australia
NATIONALITY: Australian
YEARS ACTIVE: 2011-24
TEAMS: HRT (2011), Toro Rosso (2012-13), Red Bull (2014-18), Renault (2019-20), McLaren (2021-22), AlphaTauri (2023), RB (2024)
FIRST ENTRY: 2011 British Grand Prix

F1 CAREER

0 F1 Championships
8 wins
32 podiums
3 pole positions

STATS & RECORDS

17 – fastest laps
3rd – highest position in the Drivers' Championship
232 – second-most consecutive race starts

IMAGES: ADOBE STOCK, GETTY

FORMULA 1 ALL-STARS

The **COOL, CALM** and **COLLECTED** Finn who triumphed in a **LEGENDARY SEASON FINALE**

KIMI RÄIKKÖNEN

Räikkönen was the bridesmaid of the early 2000s, picking up nine wins, 36 podiums and two second-place finishes in the Drivers' Championship with McLaren. That caught the eye of Ferrari bosses, and Räikkönen was selected for a seemingly impossible mission: replacing Michael Schumacher for the Prancing Horse. He was up for the task. Räikkönen started well, winning the first Grand Prix of 2007 from pole position, and ended just as impressively, winning the final two races. That last victory sealed one of the greatest season finales in F1 history. Räikkönen leapfrogged both drivers from his former team McLaren and topped the Drivers' Championship by a single point. Although unreliability plagued Ferrari after that and Räikkönen didn't win a second title, he remained a frontrunner and race winner for more than a decade and finished third in the standings on three occasions.

FAST FACT
Räikkönen was the second-highest paid athlete in the world in 2009.

KIMI RÄIKKÖNEN

THE ICEMAN'S DEBUT

Räikkönen was awarded a seat at Sauber despite only having 23 races in Formula Ford and Formula Renault under his belt, yet he still guided his car to sixth place to score his first Formula 1 point. It later emerged that Räikkönen had been napping 30 minutes before the race began. The Iceman had arrived.

BIO

DATE OF BIRTH: 17 October 1979
BIRTHPLACE: Espoo, Finland
NATIONALITY: Finnish
YEARS ACTIVE: 2001-09, 2012-21
TEAMS: Sauber (2001), McLaren (2002-06), Ferrari (2007-09), Lotus (2012-13), Ferrari (2014-18), Alfa Romeo (2019-21)
FIRST ENTRY: 2001 Australian Grand Prix

F1 CAREER

1 F1 Championship (2007)
21 wins
103 podiums
18 pole positions

STATS & RECORDS

72 – most podiums not starting from front row
10 – joint-most fastest laps in a season
45 – most third-place finishes

IMAGES: ADOBE STOCK, GETTY

FORMULA 1 ALL-STARS

> A stark contrast to the standard image of an F1 driver, Prost was nevertheless a **FIERCE COMPETITOR** and a **GREAT CHAMPION**

ALAIN PROST

FAST FACT
Prost was the first and (so far) only World Champion produced by France.

ALAIN PROST

A picture of concentration before the 1984 Brazilian Grand Prix

A confrontational character, with the broken nose to prove it, Prost won admirers and detractors in equal measure. Many F1 drivers are flamboyant, even reckless, but Prost approached the job in a very different manner. He was not as naturally gifted as some of his rivals, and was not able to hit the speeds the fastest racers reached – but he could out-think them and out-plan them, and his careful, methodical racing brought him four Drivers' Championships... and a nickname.

'The Professor' drove thoughtfully, nursing his car through the early stages of races and saving himself for a charge at the end. Nobody could ever doubt his method – his 51 Grand Prix victories were a record when he retired in 1993 – but he had a combative side. He fell out with his team on numerous occasions, as well as getting embroiled in the most famous rivalry in F1 history, with his polar opposite, Ayrton Senna.

BIO

DATE OF BIRTH: 24 February 1955
BIRTHPLACE: Lorette, France
NATIONALITY: French
YEARS ACTIVE: 1980-91, 1993
TEAMS: McLaren (1980), Renault (1981-83), McLaren (1984-89), Ferrari (1990-91), Williams (1993)
FIRST ENTRY: 1980 Argentine Grand Prix

F1 CAREER

4 F1 Championships (1985, 1986, 1989, 1993)
51 wins
106 podiums
33 pole positions

STATS & RECORDS

4 – joint-most runners-up finishes in the Drivers' Championship

6 – most wins at the Brazilian Grand Prix

81.25% – joint-second highest percentage of pole positions in a season

IMAGES: ADOBE STOCK, GETTY

DID YOU KNOW?
Prost scored eight 'hat-tricks' – pole position, win, and fastest lap in the same race.

LATE BLOOMER

>>> Unlike many F1 greats, driving was not Prost's first love. He was active in many sports as a youngster (breaking that famous nose several times) and only dipped his toe into motorsports at the age of 14. He quickly fell in love with karting and he became a full-time driver in 1974, moving up to Formula Renault in 1976 (pictured).

CONTRACT KILLER

>>> Prost would develop a reputation for being difficult to work with, and he broke his first contract in F1, with McLaren, after just one year, citing a lack of confidence in the car and the team. Several crashes had left him nursing injuries and he decided a jump to Renault was in his best interests.

IMAGES: ADOBE STOCK, GETTY

ALAIN PROST

HOMETOWN HERO

›› A first win in F1 is always special – for Prost it was even more so as it came at Dijon, in his home Grand Prix in 1981. Afterwards, he spoke of the confidence boost that came with winning a race at the highest level: "Before, you thought you could do it. Now you know you can."

> "Prost would develop a reputation for being difficult to work with"

WIN AT ALL COSTS

›› Prost's rivalry with Ayrton Senna reached a peak in 1989 and 1990 – in consecutive seasons, at the Japanese Grand Prix, the two great drivers collided with each other. In 1989, the crash (pictured) handed Prost his third World Championship. The following year, it was Senna who won the title after the two came together on the very first corner at Suzuka.

FORMULA 1 ALL-STARS

*Meet the **MEXICAN BATTLER** and **MASTER OVERTAKER***

SERGIO PÉREZ

Off the grid, Pérez was happy to play a supporting role to Max Verstappen. On the grid, he could be a fiery competitor. Pérez's ability to punch his way through the pack was honed during his first few years when he drove uncompetitive cars for Sauber, McLaren and Force India. However, Pérez's career turned a corner after Force India rebranded as Racing Point and found an extra turn of speed. Pérez's fourth-place Drivers' Championship finish and maiden race win caught the eye of Red Bull, who recruited him to partner young gun Verstappen. Although Pérez was usually outdriven by his teammate, he retained the ability to battle for position. In 2023, Pérez set an F1 record for the most overtakes in a season with 95. Although he parted ways with Red Bull and F1 at the end of 2024, don't be surprised if he's back on the grid before long.

FAST FACT
Pérez is eighth on the all-time Grand Prix starts lists.

SERGIO PÉREZ

RECORD-BREAKING WIN

Pérez took advantage of an unusually poor showing from Mercedes and Red Bull to romp to victory in the 2020 Sakhir Grand Prix in Bahrain. Although his car spun on the first lap, Pérez clawed his way back to second and benefitted when a botched pit stop left leader George Russell with a puncture. No driver had entered more races before claiming their first win.

BIO

DATE OF BIRTH: 26 January 1990
BIRTHPLACE: Guadalajara, Mexico
NATIONALITY: Mexican
YEARS ACTIVE: 2011-24
TEAMS: Sauber (2011-12), McLaren (2013), Force India/Racing Point (2014-20), Red Bull (2021-24)
FIRST ENTRY: 2011 Australian Grand Prix

F1 CAREER

0 F1 Championships
6 wins
39 podiums
3 pole positions

STATS & RECORDS

194 – most races before a race win

1,638 – second-most career points without being World Champion

219 – most races before a pole position

IMAGES: ADOBE STOCK, GETTY

FORMULA 1 ALL-STARS

The THREE-TIME CHAMPION and safety campaigner who CHANGED F1 FOR THE BETTER

JACKIE STEWART

FAST FACT
Stewart's 27 wins worked out at exactly 27% of the races he entered.

JACKIE STEWART

THE TIRELESS CAMPAIGNER

Stewart made his debut at the height of F1's most dangerous era. Cars were more powerful than ever, but safety precautions didn't keep up. After several friends were killed in accidents, Stewart became the drivers' greatest advocate. He pushed for the adoption of better barriers, seat belts, run-off areas and full-face helmets, and chose not to compete at his final Grand Prix after the death of his teammate François Cevert in qualifying.

Stewart made his F1 Championship debut for BRM and secured an impressive third place in his first season, but he really started flying when his old friend Ken Tyrrell decided to dip his toe into Formula 1. They immediately formed a productive partnership. Tyrrell had a decade's experience building racing cars for junior formulae, while Stewart was a skilled tactician behind the wheel who brought the best out of Tyrrell's engineering. Stewart finished second in the standings in Tyrrell's inaugural season, then powered to an easy championship victory in 1969, winning six of 11 races. He added another six wins on his way to the title again in 1971, then five more wins in 1973 to take his third title in five years. Stewart retired not just a treble world champion but a crusader who left the sport in a better condition than it was when he started.

BIO

DATE OF BIRTH: 11 June 1939
BIRTHPLACE: Milton, Scotland
NATIONALITY: British
YEARS ACTIVE: 1965-73
TEAMS: BRM (1965-67), Tyrrell (1968-73)
FIRST ENTRY: 1965 South African Grand Prix

F1 CAREER

3 F1 Championships (1969, 1971, 1973)
27 wins
43 podiums
17 pole positions

STATS & RECORDS

15 – fastest laps
6 – consecutive seasons with a win
1,919 – total laps led

IMAGES: ADOBE STOCK, GETTY

FORMULA 1 ALL-STARS

TOP 10 F1 TEAMS

RED BULL

>>> Red Bull Racing quickly became a major force in the sport after the energy drink manufacturer decided that Formula 1 fitted its high-octane brand values perfectly. Thanks to cars designed by chassis expert Adrian Newey and a pipeline of elite driver talent, Red Bull have enjoyed two periods of domination with Sebastian Vettel and Max Verstappen.

RENAULT

>>> Although French manufacturer Renault have supplied engines to countless teams over the years, the company has had a works team in Formula 1 on two occasions. The first, between 1977 and 1985, saw Renault adopt the first turbocharged power unit. Renault returned to F1 in 2002, and it still races today under the name of Renault's sports car brand, Alpine.

MERCEDES

>>> Long before Lewis Hamilton won seven Drivers' Championships in a Mercedes, Juan Manuel Fangio had taken two titles in a car run by the German manufacturer. The team's recent success came down to a dominant engine that squeezed the maximum power from regulations that required teams to run turbocharged hybrid engines, and it led to a record eight consecutive Constructors' Championships.

COOPER

>>> Perhaps the least well-known of F1's championship-winning teams, Cooper was the brainchild of father and son Charles and John Cooper. They innovated by moving the engine to the back of their car, and it led to Drivers' and Constructors' Championship titles in 1959 and 1960. Cooper left Formula 1 in 1969, and now many have forgotten the influential role that the British outfit once had on the sport.

LOTUS

>>> Lotus boss Colin Chapman was a revolutionary car designer. He introduced full monocoque construction and a semi-reclined driving position to Formula 1, creating a car that handled better than anything on the grid and powered Lotus to seven Constructors' titles. Lotus cars tended to be fragile too, however, and several drivers were killed or injured while driving for the team.

TOP 10 F1 TEAMS

From the PRANCING HORSE to the FIGHTING BULLS, these are the MOST SUCCESSFUL TEAMS IN F1 HISTORY

MCLAREN
›› The second-oldest F1 team and the oldest independent outfit, McLaren have enjoyed their fair share of success over the years. Most came during the 1980s with Alain Prost and Ayrton Senna behind the wheel and Ron Dennis directing the team from the paddock. Since then, championships have been harder to come by, although Zak Brown has led a recent resurgence.

BENETTON
›› French clothing manufacturer Benetton had a successful foray into Formula 1 during the mid-1990s, although the team was based in the UK. Benetton's golden period saw Michael Schumacher account for 19 of the team's 27 race wins on the way to winning two Drivers' Championships, although the team didn't last long after Schumacher's departure in 1996.

BRABHAM

›› Australian racing driver Jack Brabham set up his own team in 1960, debuting in Formula 1 in 1962. Four years later he won the Drivers' and Constructors' Championships at the wheel of his own car. Denny Hulme won the title the following year, and a second period of success followed in the 1980s under Nelson Piquet. Brabham was also Bernie Ecclestone's entry point into F1 before the team folded in 1992.

FERRARI
›› The most famous and oldest surviving team on the Formula 1 grid, Italian sports car manufacturer Ferrari has competed in every F1 Championship. Perhaps it should be no surprise that they've also enjoyed the most success, with 16 Constructors' Championships and 15 Drivers' titles going to legendary names like Juan Manuel Fangio, Niki Lauda and Michael Schumacher.

WILLIAMS
›› Frank Williams' independent team punched well above its weight in the 1980s and 1990s, when they were regular contenders and nine-time Constructors' champions. Seven different drivers have won their championship in a Williams, including Nigel Mansell who dominated in 1992 thanks to the aerodynamic gains on Adrian Newey's chassis. Recent success has been harder to come by, however.

IMAGES: ADOBE STOCK, GETTY

FORMULA 1 ALL-STARS

The Monégasque who has **FULFILLED HALF OF HIS DESTINY** – but has a **BIGGER TARGET TO REACH**

CHARLES LECLERC

Charles Leclerc had a rapid rise into the upper echelons of Formula 1. Having dominated GP3 and Formula 2, Leclerc earned a seat with Sauber in 2018 and comprehensively outperformed teammate Marcus Ericsson. That drew admiring glances from Ferrari, who brought him in to partner four-time World Champion Sebastian Vettel. Leclerc did more than just partner Vettel – he beat him. Leclerc outqualified the German, earned more poles, race wins and finished fourth to Vettel's sixth. That was a phenomenal achievement and highlighted his exceptional talent. He repeated the trick in 2020 during a tough season for Ferrari, before Vettel was replaced by Carlos Sainz. Another poor team season followed, but in the last few years he has dragged Ferrari back into regular contention for race wins and podium places, if not quite a Drivers' or Constructors' Championship. A career highlight was finally winning in Monaco after years of disappointment, but a title, while running alongside seven-time champion Lewis Hamilton, is well within Leclerc's talents.

FAST FACT
Leclerc's father Hervé was also a racing driver who competed in Formula 3.

16
CHARLES LECLERC

BIO

DATE OF BIRTH: 16 October 1997
BIRTHPLACE: Monte Carlo, Monaco
NATIONALITY: Monégasque
YEARS ACTIVE: 2018-present
TEAMS: Sauber (2018), Ferrari (2019-present)
FIRST ENTRY: 2018 Australian Grand Prix

F1 CAREER

0 F1 Championships
8 wins
43 podiums
26 pole positions

STATS & RECORDS

21 YEARS, 320 DAYS – third-youngest F1 race winner

21 YEARS, 165 DAYS – second-youngest polesitter

26 – most poles without a Drivers' Championship

IMAGES: ADOBE STOCK, GETTY

DID YOU KNOW?
Leclerc's godfather was French former Formula 1 driver Jules Bianchi.

HOME RACE HEARTACHES

>>> For a while it seemed like Leclerc was destined never to win his home Grand Prix. He had DNFs in 2018 and 2019, there was no Monaco GP in 2020 due to the Covid-19 pandemic, he claimed pole in 2021 but a gearbox issue meant he didn't start the race. Then in 2022, team strategy errors cost him the race from the lead once again.

LECLERC'S MONACO DESTINY

>>> After so many frustrating failures, some were starting to believe Leclerc would never win his home race. However, 2024 rolled around and finally the stars aligned. Leclerc had an imperious weekend, claiming a comfortable pole position, then controlling the race from the front, ignoring red flags and crossing the line first to fulfil every Monégasque's dream.

IMAGES: ADOBE STOCK, GETTY

CHARLES LECLERC

A FAMILY AFFAIR

>>> History was made at the Yas Marina Circuit in Abu Dhabi in December 2024 as Leclerc took part in a practice session alongside… Leclerc. Charles, fresh from finishing third in the Drivers' Championship, took to the circuit alongside younger brother Arthur, who is a development driver for Ferrari. It's the first time siblings have shared a circuit for the same team in Formula 1.

> "Finally the stars aligned – Leclerc had an imperious weekend"

FAST START GETS MAXED OUT

>>> Ferrari – and Leclerc in particular – had a great start to 2022. Leclerc won two of the first three races, while reigning champion Max Verstappen suffered two DNFs. Leclerc had a 46-point lead, but then it all went wrong. Verstappen won five of the next six and 15 in total to overturn the biggest deficit in Formula 1 history and claim the title. Leclerc would finish a distant 2nd.

FORMULA 1 ALL-STARS

Jim Clark **STANDS HIGH** in the pantheon of **ALL-TIME GREAT** racing drivers

JIM CLARK

FAST FACT
Clark won the 1964 Saloon Car Championship by winning all eight races.

JIM CLARK

ANYTHING ON WHEELS

A notable quality of Clark's was his ability to drive anything, from tourers to rally cars, to American open-wheel racers. He won the Indy 500 in 1965 (left), when he led for 190 of the 200 laps at a then-record speed of 150mph (240kph) and would race any car, anywhere. Ironically it was an F2 rather than F1 race at Hockenheimring, the famous German circuit, where Clark's car hit a tree and he died almost instantly.

Scotsman Jim Clark was one of the greatest motor racing drivers of all time. Juan Manuel Fangio, himself usually afforded the GOAT (Greatest of All Time) mantle, acclaimed Clark as the greatest driver ever, while many of his contemporaries considered him their spiritual leader. He should have won the World Championship in 1964 and 1967, as well as the two times he did win, but while Lotus had the fastest car, it was far from the most reliable, so Clark was beaten by drivers with fewer race wins but greater consistency over a season. He was certainly the smoothest driver, never having to force a car to do what he wanted but rather caressing and gently persuading it to do so. His memorial at the Hockenheimring and his grave in Chirnside, Scotland, are both modest affairs, in keeping with his humble nature once out of a car.

BIO

DATE OF BIRTH: 4 March 1936
BIRTHPLACE: Kilmany, Scotland
NATIONALITY: British
YEARS ACTIVE: 1960-68
TEAMS: Lotus (1960-68)
FIRST ENTRY: 1960 Dutch Grand Prix

F1 CAREER

2 F1 Championships (1963, 1965)
25 race wins
32 podiums
33 pole positions

STATS & RECORDS

4min 54sec – amount of time he won the 1963 Belgian Grand Prix by

8 – most Grand Slams (pole, fastest lap, race win, led every lap of race)

100% – joint-highest percentage of possible points in a season

IMAGES: ADOBE STOCK, GETTY

FORMULA 1 ALL-STARS

The **YOUNG GUN** with the unenviable task of **REPLACING A LEGEND**

KIMI ANTONELLI

Rising star Kimi Antonelli is one of the most promising talents in single-seater racing, and with a seat at Mercedes for his debut F1 season, he's in a position to immediately make his mark on the sport. Antonelli has been entrusted with filling a big void, however – replacing multiple World Champion Lewis Hamilton. Like Hamilton, Antonelli began karting at a young age. Mercedes signed him to their driver development programme at 12 years old, by which point Antonelli had already achieved several podiums against older drivers. Under the tutelage of Mercedes instructors, Antonelli went on to win back-to-back European titles in a kart, then moved on to more powerful single-seaters. He continued to impress in Formula 4, Formula 3 and Formula 2, and he's finally got a chance to drive a Formula 1 car. His performances have earned him the right to compete on the biggest stage, and he's already tipped as a potential champion.

FAST FACT
Antonelli is the second driver, after George Russell, to graduate from the Mercedes driver development programme and drive for the Mercedes F1 team.

12

KIMI ANTONELLI

AN EVENTFUL DEBUT

Race fans saw the best and worst of Antonelli during his Formula 1 debut in the 2024 Italian Grand Prix free practice. Antonelli blasted around Monza to set the fastest lap of the session, but the car lent to him by Mercedes regular George Russell was left the worse for wear after Antonelli spun at the Curva Alboreto corner ten minutes into the session.

BIO

DATE OF BIRTH: 25 August 2006
BIRTHPLACE: Bologna, Italy
NATIONALITY: Italian
YEARS ACTIVE: 2025-present
TEAMS: Mercedes (2025-present)
FIRST ENTRY: N/A

F1 CAREER

0 F1 Championships
0 wins
0 podiums
0 pole positions

STATS & RECORDS

2 – Karting European Championships

2 – Formula 2 race wins

2 – Formula 3 regional championships

IMAGES: ADOBE STOCK, GETTY

FORMULA 1 ALL-STARS

The AUSSIE HERO who was the ULTIMATE COMBINATION OF DRIVER AND MECHANIC
JACK BRABHAM

Brabham was as happy with his head under the bonnet as he was behind the wheel. His first championship came in 1959 in a car that he helped to design: a small, mid-engined Cooper. It was a radical new look that leapfrogged the front-engined German and Italian teams and marked the moment when British engineering first left its mark on Formula 1. Cooper's mechanics weren't perfect, however, and Brabham finished the last race of the season pushing his car over the line after running out of petrol. He won five consecutive races to retain the title in 1960, then formed his own team for 1962. Brabham Racing became the premier racing car constructor of the 1960s, and in 1966, Brabham won four races on the trot to take the Drivers' Championship. He finished second to teammate Denny Hulme in 1967 but could console himself in the knowledge that his eponymous team had won the Constructors' Championship for the second year in a row.

12 JACK BRABHAM

FAST FACT
Brabham is the only driver to win the championship while driving for his own team.

JOINT RACING IN GERMANY
Brabham effectively sealed the 1966 championship with his fourth consecutive victory of the season, but the German Grand Prix wasn't just remarkable for that. The race organisers allowed Formula 2 cars to race alongside their F1 counterparts, although neither formula was allowed to score points in the other's championship. It made no difference to the end result – Brabham romped to victory again and ended the weekend with more than double the championship points of his nearest rival.

BIO
DATE OF BIRTH: 2 April 1926
BIRTHPLACE: Hurstville, Australia
NATIONALITY: Australian
YEARS ACTIVE: 1955-70
TEAMS: Cooper (1955), Brabham (1956), Walker (1957), Cooper (1957-61), Brabham (1962-70)
FIRST ENTRY: 1955 British Grand Prix

F1 CAREER
3 F1 Championships (1959, 1960, 1966)
14 wins
31 podiums
13 pole positions

STATS & RECORDS
12 – fastest laps

847km – consecutive distance led in 1960

5 – consecutive race wins in 1960

IMAGES: ADOBE STOCK, GETTY

FORMULA 1 ALL-STARS

GERMANY'S WUNDERKIND embraced the life of an F1 driver like few before him, living, breathing and **LOVING THE SPORT**

SEBASTIAN VETTEL

One of the first trophies Sebastian Vettel won, as a young go-karter, was handed to him by Michael Schumacher. It was a promising omen, but there was already little doubt that racing would be in the boy's future. Vettel grew up quickly and he was a full-time F1 driver, while still a teenager, with Toro Rosso. While many drivers (and teenagers) are moody and inscrutable, Vettel won hearts from the start with his big smile and quick humour. Here was a young man who clearly loved what he was doing, and the racing world loved him for it. As a sometimes rash young driver, Vettel had his share of incidents, including a collision with Mark Webber at Fuji in 2008, but he matured quickly, winning four consecutive Drivers' Championships from 2010 to 2013 and registering the fourth-highest number of Grand Prix victories, marking him out as one of the greats.

FAST FACT
Vettel did not top the Drivers' Championship standings in 2010 until the final race of the season.

SEBASTIAN VETTEL
5

Vettel at Hockenheim in 2010

BIO

DATE OF BIRTH: 3 July 1987

BIRTHPLACE: Heppenheim, Germany

NATIONALITY: German

YEARS ACTIVE: 2007-22

TEAMS: BMW Sauber (2006-07), Toro Rosso (2007-08), Red Bull (2009-14), Ferrari (2015-20), Aston Martin (2021-22)

FIRST ENTRY: 2007 United States Grand Prix

F1 CAREER

4 F1 Championships (2010, 2011 2012, 2013)

53 wins

122 podiums

57 pole positions

STATS & RECORDS

23 YEARS 134 DAYS – youngest World Drivers' Champion

15 – most pole positions in a season

21 YEARS 72 DAYS – youngest pole position winner

IMAGES: ADOBE STOCK, GETTY

FORMULA 1 ALL-STARS

DID YOU KNOW?
Although a fearless driver, Vettel has admitted to being afraid of mice.

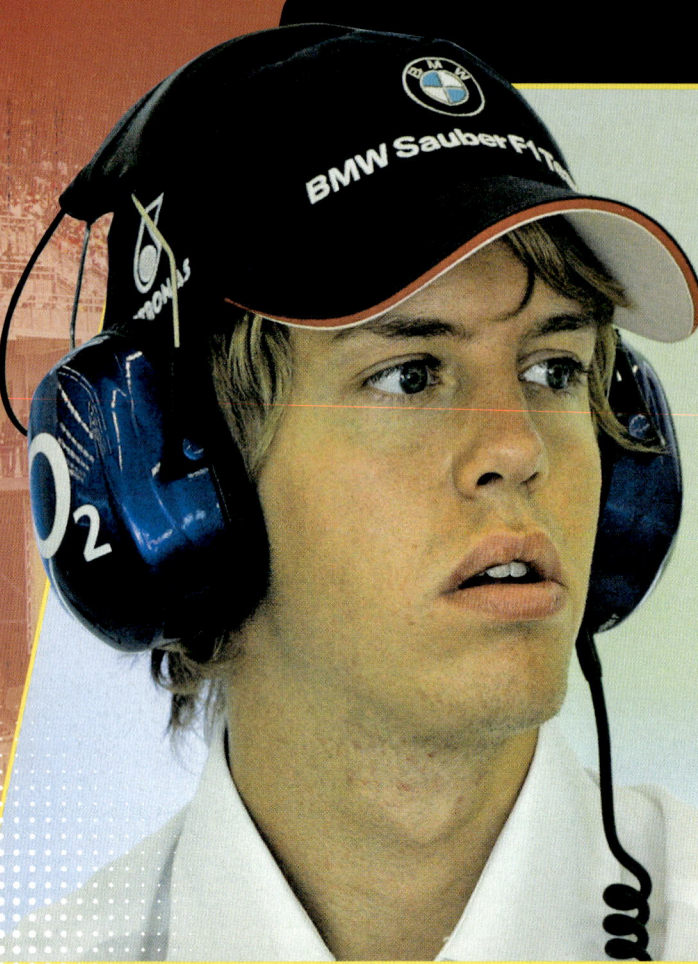

YOUNG GUN

>>> It was clear that Vettel was a precocious talent from the start. After falling in love with go-karting at the age of three and a half, he was racing in the German Formula BMW Championship at 17, winning 18 out of 20 races to completely dominate the competition. Two years later, in 2006, he was a test driver for BMW Sauber.

"It was clear that Vettel was a precocious talent from the start"

TAKING HIS CHANCE

>>> Vettel's big break in F1 came after an injury to Robert Kubica. Vettel took his place in the 2007 United States Grand Prix at Indianapolis and raised eyebrows by qualifying in seventh place on the grid. He proved that was no fluke by finishing eighth, becoming the youngest driver ever to earn a championship point.

IMAGES: ADOBE STOCK, GETTY

SEBASTIAN VETTEL

SINGING IN THE RAIN

>>> After switching to Toro Rosso, the 2008 season brought glory for Vettel. Although still finding his feet in the sport, he won pole position at Monza. Defying the wet conditions, he went on to win his first Grand Prix, and the first for Toro Rosso. At 21 years and 73 days old, he was the youngest driver ever to win a Grand Prix.

A LEGEND BOWS OUT

>>> Vettel announced he would be retiring at the end of the 2022 season and his fellow drivers showed how much they thought of him by holding a special dinner in his honour prior to the last race of his career, with Lewis Hamilton acting as host. On the starting grid the next day, the other drivers formed a guard of honour to show their respect for one of the greatest drivers the sport has ever seen.

FORMULA 1 ALL-STARS

THE FLYING FINN whose **CAREER TOOK OFF** in the last years of the millennium

MIKA HÄKKINEN

After cutting his teeth for two years with Lotus, Mika Häkkinen was chosen to partner Ayrton Senna at McLaren in 1993. Unfortunately, team principal Ron Dennis dropped Häkkinen during pre-season testing in favour of Michael Andretti, and Häkkinen was left in the wilderness as McLaren's test driver. He was given a three-race stint at the end of the season though, and a single podium was enough to keep the seat full-time in 1994. He won his first Grand Prix in the final race of 1997 – helped by champion Jacques Villeneuve moving aside and teammate David Coulthard voluntarily giving up first place – but Häkkinen needed no charity in the season that followed. He won eight races and his first Drivers' Championship, and he retained the title in 1999. The Flying Finn bowed out of Formula 1 after 2001 with 20 wins in 11 years, all in the second half of his career.

FAST FACT
Häkkinen won his first race at the 99th time of asking.

14 MIKA HÄKKINEN

HORROR CRASH DOWN UNDER

Häkkinen was coming to the end of his fifth season in F1 when his McLaren ran over debris in qualifying for the 1995 Australian Grand Prix. After losing control with a catastrophic puncture, Häkkinen's car slammed into the wall at sickening speed. Doctors were on the scene in seconds and found Häkkinen had a blocked airway, but they acted fast to carry out a trackside tracheotomy that saved his life.

BIO

DATE OF BIRTH: 28 September 1968
BIRTHPLACE: Vantaa, Finland
NATIONALITY: Finnish
YEARS ACTIVE: 1991-2001
TEAMS: Lotus (1991-92), McLaren (1993-2001)
FIRST ENTRY: 1991 United States Grand Prix

F1 CAREER

2 F1 Championships (1998, 1999)
20 wins
51 podiums
26 pole positions

STATS & RECORDS

8 – seasons before first title

15 – joint-most podium finishes before first win

5 – career hat-tricks (pole, win, and fastest lap in same race)

IMAGES: ADOBE STOCK, GETTY

FORMULA 1 ALL-STARS

The **LOYAL WINGMAN** who contributed to his teammates' titles, but **NEVER WON ONE OF HIS OWN**

RUBENS BARRICHELLO

Barrichello spent seven years learning his trade with middle-of-the-grid teams before getting a drive with frontrunners Ferrari. Not until his 124th race did Barrichello finally cross the line for his maiden race win at the German Grand Prix – a victory that disappointed the home fans who wanted Barrichello's teammate Michael Schumacher to win. Schumacher fans couldn't complain too much though. Barrichello was a dependable teammate, helping the Scuderia to five Constructors' Championships and supporting Schumacher's runs to the Drivers' Championship. After joining Brawn, Barrichello played wingman again. He added valuable points to help his new team take the Constructors' title while Jenson Button romped to the Drivers' trophy. Although Barrichello never took the top prize himself, he did outperform his teammates in one regard. When he retired in 2011, Barrichello had 322 starts, but his championship-winning teammates both finished on 306.

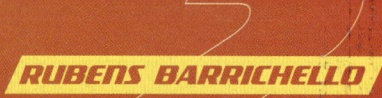

RUBENS BARRICHELLO

FAST FACT
Barrichello won the 2000 German Grand Prix despite starting 18th on the grid.

BIO
DATE OF BIRTH: 23 May 1972
BIRTHPLACE: São Paulo, Brazil
NATIONALITY: Brazilian
YEARS ACTIVE: 1993-2011
TEAMS: Jordan (1993-96), Stewart (1997-99), Ferrari (2000-05), Honda (2006-08), Brawn (2009), Williams (2010-11)
FIRST ENTRY: 1993 South African Grand Prix

F1 CAREER
0 F1 Championships
11 wins
68 podiums
14 pole positions

STATS & RECORDS
326 – most consecutive race entries
104 – most races with a single teammate (Michael Schumacher)
19 – most consecutive seasons with a start

PHOTO FINISH IN TEXAS
Barrichello's victory in the United States in 2002 was one of the closest finishes to an F1 Grand Prix. He followed teammate Michael Schumacher for most of the race, but Schumacher slowed on the last lap to allow Barrichello to pip him by 0.011 seconds. It didn't make a huge difference to overall season results, though. By then Schumacher had already secured the Drivers' Championship with Barrichello a distant second in the standings.

IMAGES: ADOBE STOCK, GETTY

FORMULA 1 ALL-STARS

*Against all odds, Jenson Button rose from **UNDERDOG TO WORLD CHAMPION**, culminating in a **FAIRY-TALE 2009 SEASON***

JENSON BUTTON

Becoming the youngest British F1 driver when he made his debut at the 2000 Australian Grand Prix in Melbourne with Williams, Jenson Button, known for his smooth racing style, didn't claim his first Grand Prix win until 2006 with Honda, at the Hungaroring circuit. Three seasons later and Button's career peaked in 2009 when he claimed the World Drivers' Championship with Brawn GP, in a year where he secured six wins in the first seven races. Life after F1 has been just as full-throttle, as the Brit competed in Japan's Super GT series, winning the 2018 title, launched his JBXE team in Extreme E, has raced full-time in the World Endurance Championship for Hertz Team Jota since 2024, works as a pundit for Sky Sports F1, and serves as a senior advisor to Williams Racing.

FAST FACT
Button was ranked as a 100/1 outsider by bookmakers the year he won the F1 Championship.

JENSON BUTTON

WET-WEATHER MASTERCLASS

Button's victory at the 2011 Canadian Grand Prix is still widely regarded as one of F1's greatest races. Lasting over four hours (due to rain delays), Button tallied up six pit stops, was involved in two collisions (with Lewis Hamilton and Fernando Alonso), and dropped to plum last, yet in a comeback like no other, he delivered a wet-weather masterclass, overtaking Sebastian Vettel on the final lap to secure the most improbable win.

BIO

DATE OF BIRTH: 19 January 1980
BIRTHPLACE: Frome, England
NATIONALITY: British
YEARS ACTIVE: 2000-17
TEAMS: Williams (2000), Benetton (2001), Renault (2002), BAR (2003-05), Honda (2006-08), Brawn (2009), McLaren (2010-17)
FIRST ENTRY: 2000 Australian Grand Prix

F1 CAREER

1 F1 Championships (2009)
15 wins
50 podiums
8 pole positions

STATS & RECORDS

10 – seasons before winning title

62.50% – percentage of poles converted to wins

179 – seventh-most consecutive race starts

FORMULA 1 ALL-STARS

He always had the ABILITY AND BELIEF, but would fate ever give Mansell a good enough car to become WORLD CHAMPION?

NIGEL MANSELL

Nigel Mansell looked the part of the typical lugubrious, rather dour Englishman. But on the track he was a warrior, a man born to race who thrived on the wheel-to-wheel, head-to-head competition. Mansell had a firm sense of his own worth, and more than once he walked away from a team rather than get embroiled in political or financial shenanigans, or negotiations that he felt were beneath him or a betrayal of a previous agreement. But Mansell never gave less than his all to any car, or any team he drove for, and the British and Italian fans adored him, while motor racing fans all over the world came to admire his whole-hearted efforts to win. Mansell's career statistics support the view he was fully deserving of his Drivers' Championship crown in 1992.

FAST FACT
Mansell is the oldest British driver to win a Grand Prix (41 years old at the 1994 Australian GP).

NIGEL MANSELL
5

Sadly, the McLarens of 1994 and 1995 were just not competitive enough to give Mansell a fairy-tale ending

BIO

DATE OF BIRTH: 8 August 1953

BIRTHPLACE: Upton-upon-Severn, England

NATIONALITY: British

YEARS ACTIVE: 1980-92, 1994-95

TEAMS: Lotus (1980-84), Williams (1985-88), Ferrari (1989-90), Williams (1991-92, 1994), McLaren (1995)

FIRST ENTRY: 1980 Austrian Grand Prix

F1 CAREER

1 F1 Championship (1992)

31 wins

59 podiums

32 pole positions

STATS & RECORDS

32 – number of races he crashed out of

3 – number of times he finished second in the Drivers' Championship

87.5% – highest percentage of pole positions in a season (1992)

IMAGES: ADOBE STOCK, GETTY

FORMULA 1 ALL-STARS

DID YOU KNOW?
Mansell broke his neck during the 1977 Formula Ford Championship and was told he'd never drive again.

THE WILLIAMS 14/14B: CAR OF THE DECADE

>>> The Adrian Newey-designed FW14 combined a sleek, highly aerodynamic package with an advanced gearbox, and the consistently dependable Renault engine took Mansell to second place in the 1991 Drivers' Championship. A few tweaks took place during the off-season, including perfecting the computer-controlled active suspension. The 14B cornered with astonishing speed and poise, allowing Mansell to win the first five races of 1992 and largely dominate the season.

MANSELL WINS CART

> "Mansell made the surprise decision to race in the CART series"

>>> Whatever the truth about the dispute between Mansell and Williams at the end of 1992, it was surely careless of the team to let a defending World Champion slip away. Instead of going to another F1 team, Mansell made the surprise decision to race in the CART series in North America, signing for Newman/Haas Racing. It was a triumph. Mansell became the only driver in history to hold the F1 and CART titles simultaneously.

IMAGES: ADOBE STOCK, GETTY

NIGEL MANSELL

THE MOVE TO FERRARI

››› When the archetypal Englishman signed for the very Italian motor racing team, the shock was almost as seismic as the one that accompanied Lewis Hamilton's move for 2025. But if it seemed like an unlikely match, the Tifosi quickly came to love the driver they christened 'Il Leone' for his whole-hearted racing style, his determination and his fearlessness. The title didn't quite come – he finished fourth and fifth in his two seasons at Ferrari – but the respect certainly did.

MANSELL v PIQUET

››› Piquet and Mansell were, it's safe to say, never good friends. In 1986 and 1987 they were Williams teammates, but with both in contention for the title it was always going to be difficult keeping them happy all the time. Mansell was nominally the number two driver but focused all his physical strength and willingness to take risks to pressurise Piquet. Both men agreed that their on-track racing always stayed fair.

FORMULA 1 ALL-STARS

TOP 10 F1 BOSSES

TOTO WOLFF

>>> Perfectionist Wolff joined Mercedes just at the right time. After three years as a mid-grid team, Mercedes gained the most from new engine regulations and suddenly transformed into the most dominant team the grid has ever seen. Wolff's a protective leader who shields his drivers from controversy, although he's been known to get into his own spats with rivals.

ROSS BRAWN

>>> As technical director at Benetton and Ferrari, Brawn was the mastermind behind the cars that won seven Constructors' Championships. Brawn stepped up to team principal for a single year in 2009 when he took over the old Honda team and ran it as the self-named Brawn GP. It was a surprise success, claiming both the Constructors' Championship and Drivers' title with Jenson Button.

KEN TYRRELL

>>> Tyrrell entered Formula 1 as team principal of the new Matra team and kept it going under his own name when Matra moved on after two seasons. Tyrrell's greatest skill was as a talent scout. He was an early advocate for Jackie Stewart, and Stewart repaid his faith by racing for most of his career in a Tyrrell.

COLIN CHAPMAN

>>> Sharp-suited and slick-haired Chapman was a talented engineer who went against the grain. When other teams were bulking up their cars to get more power, Chapman sought to cut weight and use aerodynamics to improve handling. It worked, and Lotus cars won seven Constructors' and six Drivers' Championships in the 1960s and 1970s.

CHRISTIAN HORNER

>>> Long-term boss of Red Bull Racing, Horner helped the new team establish itself in Formula 1 and recruited elite car designer Adrian Newey to build the team's vehicles. Under Horner's leadership, Red Bull's driver programme has become Formula 1's primary talent factory supplying not just Red Bull but several other teams on the grid.

TOP 10 F1 BOSSES

Part-designer, part-motivator, part-recruiter – THE DRIVING FORCE behind every great team is its principal

BERNIE ECCLESTONE

>>> Best known for running Formula 1 for 30 years, Ecclestone purchased the Brabham team in 1971. During his 15 years at the helm, Brabham won 22 races and two Drivers' Championship titles for Nelson Piquet. Ecclestone also led a huge realignment in the redistribution of power in F1 when the teams took control from the motorsport authorities.

FLAVIO BRIATORE

>>> Guiding Benetton and Renault to three Constructors' Championships, Briatore gained a reputation for pushing regulations to their limit. His teams were accused of cheating (but evaded punishment) in 1994 and 2007, but Briatore was found guilty of telling Nelson Piquet Jr to deliberately crash to help his teammate in 2008. After his lifetime ban was reduced on appeal, Briatore's now back in the F1 game.

FRANK WILLIAMS

>>> Williams was a team principal in Formula 1 for 43 years, and most of his success came in the 1980s and 1990s when the Williams racing team won nine Constructors' Championships and had seven different Drivers' titles with seven different drivers. Most of those titles were won after Williams had become wheelchair-bound following a road traffic accident in 1986.

RON DENNIS

>>> With almost 30 years as a team principal and the beneficiary of talented drivers including Ayrton Senna, Niki Lauda and Alain Prost, Dennis's era at McLaren saw the team win seven Constructors' Championships and ten Drivers' Championships. Dennis focused on minute details and he was obsessive in his pursuit of perfection, but he was also a blue-sky thinker who could predict new developments years ahead.

JEAN TODT

>>> Todt took a Ferrari team that had been struggling for more than a decade and overhauled it by poaching top talent from the best team on the grid. Todt pursued a trio of driver Michael Schumacher and designers Ross Brawn and Rory Byrne from Benetton, and together they claimed six consecutive Constructors' titles – and one more for good measure in 2007.

IMAGES: ADOBE STOCK, GETTY

FORMULA 1 ALL-STARS

Future PLC Quay House, The Ambury, Bath, BA1 1UA

Editorial
Group Editor **Dan Peel**
Senior Designer **Perry Wardell-Wicks**
Head of Art & Design **Greg Whitaker**
Editorial Director **Jon White**
Managing Director **Grainne McKenna**

Contributors
Rob Clark, Natalie Denton, Briony Duguid, Jamie Frier, Jessica Leggett, Scott Reeves, David Smith

Cover images
Adobe Stock, Getty Images

Photography
All copyrights and trademarks are recognised and respected

Advertising
Media packs are available on request
Commercial Director **Clare Dove**

International
Head of Print Licensing **Rachel Shaw**
licensing@futurenet.com
www.futurecontenthub.com

Circulation
Head of Newstrade **Tim Mathers**

Production
Head of Production **Mark Constance**
Production Project Manager **Matthew Eglinton**
Advertising Production Manager **Joanne Crosby**
Digital Editions Controller **Jason Hudson**
Production Managers **Keely Miller, Nola Cokely, Vivienne Calvert, Fran Twentyman**

Printed in the UK

Distributed by Marketforce – www.marketforce.co.uk
For enquiries, please email: mfcommunications@futurenet.com

GPSR EU RP (for authorities only)
eucomply OÜ Pärnu mnt 139b-14 11317, Tallinn, Estonia
hello@eucompliancepartner.com, +3375690241

All stats and records correct as of the end of the 2024 F1 season.

Formula 1 and related marks are trade marks of Formula One Licensing BV, a Formula 1 company. This bookazine is 100% UNOFFICIAL and in no way affiliated with Formula 1.

Formula 1 All-Stars First Edition (SBZ7008)
© 2025 Future Publishing Limited

We are committed to only using magazine paper which is derived from responsibly managed, certified forestry and chlorine-free manufacture. The paper in this bookazine was sourced and produced from sustainable managed forests, conforming to strict environmental and socioeconomic standards.

All contents © 2025 Future Publishing Limited or published under licence. All rights reserved. No part of this magazine may be used, stored, transmitted or reproduced in any way without the prior written permission of the publisher. Future Publishing Limited (company number 2008885) is registered in England and Wales. Registered office: Quay House, The Ambury, Bath BA1 1UA. All information contained in this publication is for information only and is, as far as we are aware, correct at the time of going to press. Future cannot accept any responsibility for errors or inaccuracies in such information. You are advised to contact manufacturers and retailers directly with regard to the price of products/services referred to in this publication. Apps and websites mentioned in this publication are not under our control. We are not responsible for their contents or any other changes or updates to them. This magazine is fully independent and not affiliated in any way with the companies mentioned herein.

Future plc is a public company quoted on the London Stock Exchange (symbol: FUTR)
www.futureplc.com

Chief Executive Officer **Kevin Li Ying**
Non-Executive Chairman **Richard Huntingford**
Chief Financial Officer **Sharjeel Suleman**

Tel +44 (0)1225 442 244